To Oz, Debi, D.J. & Carina

Thanks for the memories in Sedona, we had a great time! We always enjoy our time with your family.

God Bless you all

Greg, Kara, Briana & Gregory

2-15-99

SEDONA

The most uniquely beautiful site on Earth

SEDONA

The most uniquely beautiful site on Earth

Photography by Tom Johnson

Text by Hoyt C. Johnson, Publisher SEDONA MAGAZINE

SEDONA PUBLISHING COMPANY

Sedona, Arizona

For the adventurous people who experience
a strong attraction to this spectacular area,
and subsequently, become
attached to this unique
community in a very magnetic,
lasting manner.

Published by Sedona Publishing Company
P.O. Box 219, Sedona, Arizona 86339
271 Van Deren Road, Sedona, Arizona 86336
(520) 282-9022

Library of Congress Catalog Card Number 98-84593
International Standard Book Number 1-890195-04-9

Design: Pinnacle Productions, Sedona, Arizona
Color Separations: American Color, Phoenix, Arizona
Printing: Land O' Sun Printers, Scottsdale, Arizona
Binding: Roswell Bookbinding, Phoenix, Arizona

Printed in United States of America
First Printing: July 1998

CONTENTS

Sedona is a land of many dreams.

Throughout this area's history, motivated men and women have entertained ambitions inspired by spectacular natural beauty. How can anyone who experiences an exciting, adventurous romance with the canyons, rims and plateaus, forests, creeks and massive red-rock formations that characterize this land not dream a little?

Between A.D. 1130 and A.D. 1280, Native American people who were attracted to this area by its beauty, dreamed of building "world-class" cliff dwellings in exceptionally warm, fertile canyons — and they did. Six centuries later, the first man to take squatter's rights in Oak Creek Canyon, Jim Thompson, dreamed about building a road from Sedona to Indian Gardens, four miles into the canyon — and he did, around Steamboat Rock and through Wilson Canyon with a pick, shovel and dynamite.

In the very early 1900s, a group of five Sedona men obtained financing from Coconino County to build a road they had dreamed about — up Schnebly Hill, on a cattle trail originally constructed by the William Munds family. And a decade later, Frank Pendley's dream came true when he planted orchards in Oak Creek Canyon — orchards nourished by a 1.5-mile irrigation ditch most people thought could not be built. Pendley's dream occurred approximately 10 years before popular novelist Zane Grey penned a book he dreamed would be a best seller, and "The Call of the Canyon" still is being sold in bookstores.

In 1902, when Sedona Schnebly approached this area from mining-town Jerome in a horse-drawn wagon — she had traveled from Missouri to Prescott by train in order to join her husband, Carl — she had dreams, too. However, I don't think she ever dreamed that this community would be named Sedona.

The list of other notable dreamers includes Marguerite Brunswig Staude, who upon visiting St. Patrick's Cathedral in New York City in 1932, wondered why its architects had exhausted themselves copying Gothic design "instead of bravely pioneering an expression of contemporary art." On that day, she dreamed about a church, "cruciform in plan and elevation," and in 1956, she completed construction of world-famed Chapel of the Holy Cross in Sedona.

This community's list of beloved dreamers also includes Abe Miller — plus others too numerous to mention, though my purpose is to cite dreams more than dreamers. For years, Miller envisioned a very special arts and crafts village, "the first of its kind in the nation." And his dream was to create this unique facility in Sedona, which he did in the early 1970s. Today, Tlaquepaque is credited with "setting the pace and establishing the flavor of Sedona."

Sedona is full of dreamers, including the community leaders who headed the incorporation of this city in 1988, and the people who spearheaded the establishment of a local school district and construction of a new high school in 1993. I am a dreamer, too, as are my "partners" — my son, Tom, whose exceptional talent as a photographer is well-known; my wife, Marcia; and my son, John.

Yes, by the nature of our work, Tom and I were intimately associated with the creation of this book, but our dream — to successfully establish *Sedona Magazine*, and then to create a signature publication for this community — is shared with Marcia and John. Indeed, we are a very close-knit unit with overlapping and interlocking responsibilities, and they also are creators of this book.

It's easier to dream as a team.

Hoyt C. Johnson, Publisher

Rarely is a community blessed with two environments so contrasting and spectacularly beautiful —

as is Sedona, which boasts of Red Rock Country and Oak Creek Canyon.

CHAPTER ONE

No matter what direction they come from, when visitors emerge from mystic Oak Creek Canyon; suddenly confront Bell and Courthouse rocks; carefully wind down Schnebly Hill Road; or catch an unbelievable glimpse of Red Canyon and Secret Mountain, strategically situated in front of the Mogollon Rim, they are spellbound by the spectacular beauty and awesome magnitude of this area's incredible landscape. More than anything, they are stunned by the way this landscape is punctuated by massive red-rock formations that have become renowned throughout the world.

This is Red Rock Country. This is a land that features magnificent sights as unique as any natural splendor on Earth. And testifying to the insatiable curiosity of our civilization, the questions that echo throughout the enchanting canyons that give this area its distinctive character, are: "How did it happen? — and when did it happen?"

Well, *as it happened*, this unique area was positioned at the temperate base of the Mogollon Rim escarpment, which was carved by perennial Oak Creek and other Verde River tributaries. Consequently, abundant clues revealed by powerful, natural forces are offered by the same spires, buttes and mesas that cause these questions to be asked. Also, Oak Creek Canyon, eroded into the southwestern margin of the Colorado Plateau, provides a complementary exhibit of geological information.

Though some differences of opinion regarding the geologic history of Sedona's famed red rocks are yet to be resolved, it is extremely interesting to note that experts who have examined these clues and related information agree that this area's beloved landscape has been in the making for more than 350 million years. It is intriguing, too, that in many respects, the sedimentary rocks of Sedona are similar to their contemporaries in the classic, upper Grand Canyon region. Stratums in the Grand Canyon also are encountered in the Sedona area, and the correlation is simple: these layers of limestone and sandstone were deposited in very large-scale environments such as oceans and coastal deserts, which essentially negates the effect of Sedona and the Grand Canyon being located 80 miles apart.

Approximately 300 million years ago, when the land that now is Sedona was situated close to sea level, this area and the Grand Canyon region formed a large embayment on the west coast of North America. Though the ocean generally remained farther west during this time, it periodically inundated the entire Sedona-Grand Canyon embayment. Thus, the deposition of sediment was cyclical according to the transgressions and regressions of the ocean.

Briefly, when the ocean's shoreline was west of the embayment, sediment eroded from the highlands to the east and northeast was deposited in this muddy coastal plain by streams en route to the sea. In contrast, when the embayment was submerged, longshore currents moved vast amounts of sand southward along the coast and reworked it into offshore bars, shoals and beaches within the bay. Also there were periods when the sea was able to slowly deposit its own limey particles. The stratums created by this varied activity are called the Supai Group.

The sandstone, silt and conglomerates resting on the Supai Group compose another stratum called the Hermit Formation, which is the foundation for much of Sedona. Because these rocks are fairly soft and susceptible to erosion, they easily weather to form slopes with low ledges, which in many cases are the rounded "skirts" that provide a base for the lofty pinnacles that dot this area.

The spectacular red rocks that decorate the horizon of Sedona and the mouth of Oak Creek Canyon are part of the more-recently defined Schnebly Hill Formation. Named for the dramatic, towering spires along Schnebly Hill Road, this 900-foot-thick layer of rock is composed of sandstone, plus small amounts of mudstone and limestone — all beautifully decorated with a reddish pigment, ferric oxide.

Geologists trace the origin of the stratum now called the Schnebly Hill Formation to a period approximately 270 million years ago, when a slowly subsiding basin gathered and preserved sand blown into this area by prevailing northerly winds. Also, these scholars credit the presence of a 6-foot-thick, area-wide ring of gray Fort Apache limestone as evidence of the formation's coastal position, saying that this distinctive layer of erosion-resistant rock was deposited during a brief period when the basin was covered by the ocean.

Cathedral Rock, near Red Rock Crossing; Coffeepot Rock, in the canyon at the end of Soldiers Pass Road; and Mitten Ridge, east of Midgley Bridge, are among the most beloved, spectacular exposures of the Schnebly Hill Formation. The naming of these and other popular formations such as Capitol Butte, Merry-Go-Round, Rabbit Ears and Wagon Train, as well as Chimney, Lizard Head, Snoopy, Bell and Courthouse rocks is an interesting — and sometimes, very confusing — story. Indeed, this story also is amusing, because during an entire century, Sedona's landmarks have been given proper names and nicknames, been renamed, and have been identified with wrong names on maps. To make matters worse, old-timers say that new residents and visitors who don't know the name of a rock, call it whatever they want.

Trying to keep track of names that are similar — like Steamboat, Submarine and Ship rocks — adds to the confusion posed by this amusing challenge, too. For example: Long ago, Courthouse Rock was called Church Rock — and Cathedral Rock was called Court Rock. There still are people here who are not pleased that these names were changed and refined. Nonetheless, with regard to Cathedral Rock, it generally is accepted that as a church figuratively opens its arms to all people, this great monument of rock embraces hikers who climb into its nave.

As a footnote, it also generally is conceded that Sedona is a better name for this community than its really old, original moniker, Camp Garden — though admittedly, these names have nothing to do with red rocks!

Up close, from a ledge on Ship Rock.

From afar, a sunset view of Ship Rock.

Massive rock formations in Red Canyon.

Earth Angel Spire in Mormon Wash.

Red Rock Secret Mountain Wilderness Area from under Devil's Bridge.

Vultee Arch north of Wilson Mountain and below Sterling Pass.

High desert wildflowers, cactus and agave.

White yucca blossoms, bursting with pride and beauty.

Evidence of welcome, summer thunderstorms.

Red Rock Country from the Mogollon Rim.

Ship and Steamboat rocks, docked in a natural, red-rock harbor.

Bell Rock, in Village of Oakcreek.

Coffeepot Rock, in north Sedona.

Snoopy Rock, in uptown Sedona.

Cathedral Rock, at Red Rock Crossing.

Cathedral Rock on a serene, fall day —

and from Schuerman Mountain.

No matter what the season —

the majesty of Cathedral Rock is impressive.

On rare occasions, Sedona "dresses up" for winter.

Low clouds add mist and mystery.

From Schnebly Hill Road, Teapot Rock is the sentinel of Bear Wallow Canyon.

CHAPTER TWO

Make no mistake; in the rest of the world, "the canyon" might mean the massive Grand Canyon, but not in this part of northern Arizona. Here, *the canyon* refers to beautiful Oak Creek Canyon, which extends northward from Sedona to a scenic overlook on top of the switchbacks that zigzag up steep, rock walls that mark the Mogollon Rim. At the overlook, this 12-mile canyon is approximately 1,500 feet deep — and near Sedona, where it merges with the northeastern margin of the vast Verde Valley, it approaches a depth of almost 2,500 feet. Interestingly, a "recent" fault — only a million years ago! — caused the canyon's west rim to rise as much as 500 feet above its east rim. And from rim to rim, Oak Creek Canyon averages a mile in width.

More than 60 years ago, members of the National Geographic Society proclaimed the highway running through Oak Creek Canyon "the most beautiful drive in America." The writer who reported this proclamation stated: "Sedona's red-rock setting is at the mouth of Oak Creek Canyon, the start of a drive never to be forgotten as travelers wind along the banks of Oak Creek, high above the swiftly rushing stream below."

Indeed, every rock-bordered curve, every tree-formed tunnel, every climbing turn of the road through this awesome canyon features more natural beauty than the one before. The romance that shrouds this spectacular area fairly hangs from the huge, creek-side cottonwoods and sycamores, just as do the grapevines in an unbelievable, adjacent vent, West Fork. This junglelike side canyon is a land where "cold sinks" — areas where cool air from the high plateau above is trapped within steep, narrow canyon walls — encourage high-elevation conifers such as ponderosa pines, Douglas firs and white firs to coexist with water-loving, lowland cottonwoods and sycamores that shade cozy, creek-side hideaways.

Geologically, Oak Creek Canyon exhibits the layers of sandstone, limestone and mudstone that compose the Supai Group. Also, spectacular examples of the Schnebly Hill Formation are prominent in areas of the canyon nearest Sedona. Higher in the canyon, however, sheer rock walls extend into the Coconino Sandstone Formation, the preserved remains of huge, wind-blown sand dunes, and the Toroweap Formation, which is displayed as orange cliffs more than 300 feet thick. Ten million years after the next stratum — a limestone layer called the Kaibab Formation — was deposited, molten lava oozed through cracks in the surface of this formation, and when this lava cooled, it formed a distinct basalt cap over the upper regions of Oak Creek Canyon. In some places, successive flows piled up, one on top of the other, to form massive, vertical columns up to 30 feet in height.

Today, before travelers cross historic Midgley Bridge at a point where powerful washes off Wilson Mountain empty into Oak Creek, they note a sign designating the next 12 miles as Oak Creek Recreation Area — and a spectacular recreation area it is, with great hiking, good fishing, convenient camping and a natural water slide at Slide Rock State Park. Especially, there are fantastic hiking trails that range from easy paths that hug the creek to moderate trails that penetrate almost-hidden side canyons to difficult climbs up steep canyon walls. More than anything else, however, Oak Creek Canyon is a sanctuary where abundant wildlife thrives amid thick vegetation. Chances are, there is not a richer, more varied and beautiful riparian area in the country.

Imagine magnificent, towering red-rock formations; a refreshing, perennial creek born of springs high in protective rock walls; surprising displays of wildflowers, berries and apple blossoms; mountain lions, coyotes, javelina and deer, as well as myriad birds, from eagles to orioles — all in a magnificent four-seasons setting featuring white, foaming waterfalls in the spring; warm days and peaceful, cool nights in the summer; long-lasting, wildly colored leaves in the fall; and short-lived, delicate decorations of snow in the winter. This is Oak Creek Canyon, where almost eight decades ago, Zane Grey penned the words that pinpoint this wonder's simple essence.

In his popular novel "Call of the Canyon" — later, a motion picture — Grey had his adventurous hero write the following words in a letter to his Eastern lover: "I never understood anything of the meaning of nature until I lived under these looming, stone walls and whispering pines."

It is this revelation — the meaning of nature — that today, still is the call of the canyon.

Rejoice! It's spring in Oak Creek Canyon.

Inviting, almost-hidden swimming holes dot Oak Creek Canyon.

Sometimes torrent —

sometimes tranquil, always precious Oak Creek.

Fall colors enhance the charm of Allen's Bend Trail —

as well as the lush, riparian areas farther into Oak Creek Canyon.

Midgley Bridge, which locals affectionately call "Midgley Bridgely."

Spectacular, exciting switchbacks at the top of Oak Creek Canyon.

Sunny, fall days in alluring Oak Creek Canyon are spectacular!

If only these giant cottonwoods could talk!

The "looming, stone walls" cited in Zane Grey's "Call of the Canyon."

Sometimes in the canyon —

seasons change overnight.

60

Probably, there will be no swimming at Slide Rock State Park on this day.

Chapter Three

Unusual attention is focused on Sedona's majestic, monolithic red-rock formations and on the immediate presence of riparian-rich Oak Creek Canyon, which is so ideally located. There is, however, another awesome product of this area's unique, physical evolution that also ignites universal acclamation. Indeed, it's as though "in the beginning," the world's master planner favored Sedona and showered treats on this land in a way that almost was unfair.

Some parts of our nation are blessed with impressive mountains, or lofty pinnacles, buttes and mesas; some boast of winding rivers, or splashing creeks; others are positioned at just the right elevation for wonderful, four-seasons climate, or situated at the intersection of a latitude and longitude bathed with 300 days of sunshine each year. Sedona was given all these amenities — and more. It also has a rim, a bold and rugged escarpment that towers over the entire eastern edge of this town. In fact, this magnificent rim, formed millions of years ago by massive uplifts and subsequent carving caused by powerful erosion, runs diagonally across north-central Arizona for 200 miles.

If through some miracle, it was possible to pick up a community and place it at another location, nobody would touch Sedona. It's in exactly the right spot, and part of the reason why it's "just right" is the presence of the Mogollon Rim, which marks the abrupt and dramatic end of the vast Colorado Plateau that covers parts of four states. Of course, the presence of an exceptional collection of geological attractions such as the Mogollon (just say "muggy-own") Rim; massive, red-rock formations; Oak Creek and its amazing canyon; and the 13,000-foot San Francisco Peaks, statuesquely situated just 35 miles north, can be explained partially by the action of related geophysical forces. Nonetheless, this city's fortuitous site is a classic example of unbelievable happenstance.

The Mogollon Rim absolutely is a geological, biological and historical treasure. As much as Oak Creek Canyon offers flora and fauna that contrast with the high-desert plant and animal life of Sedona, the Mogollon Rim exhibits much greater variety. Its climate, too, is a much-appreciated diversity, affording residents and visitors the opportunity to enjoy winter recreation within minutes of the canyon. And with regard to the rim's colorful past, historians have called it "a rich kaleidoscope of prehistoric peoples, Apache and Yavapai tribes, miners and prospectors, soldiers, cattlemen and sheepmen, outlaws, bloody feuds, great aspirations and shattered dreams."

With tongue in cheek, however, many people call the rim's unmatched qualification as an ideal site for enjoying magnificent, panoramic views of Red Rock Country as its real "claim to fame." Locals and regular visitors couldn't imagine not being able to travel up twisting, dusty Schnebly Hill Road to the top of the Mogollon Rim — a vertical rise of 2,000-plus feet — to celebrate breathtaking views of Sedona and beyond, all the way to the Verde Valley, where the charismatic, old mining town of Jerome literally hangs on Mingus Mountain. What would we do without our rim, with its cool forests, flowering meadows, sparkling lakes, bubbling brooks and mesmerizing hiking trails?

Yes, hikers who climb from the high desert around Sedona and from the floor of Oak Creek Canyon to the top of the Mogollon Rim definitely are spellbound by what they see. For example, from the top of Thomas Point Trail, a steep path up the east wall of Oak Creek Canyon, hikers are stunned by the majesty of the San Francisco Peaks at Flagstaff when they look north; turning to the south, they are awed by the steep, red-rock canyon walls surrounding Slide Rock State Park; to the east, past where Thomas Point juts over the canyon 800 feet below, they see where the Mogollon Rim and Colorado Plateau seem to extend forever; and upon facing west, these hikers are amazed by the beauty of West Fork, an expansive vent where centuries of continuous erosion wonderfully unmasked this spectacular land.

Significant events that mark the early development of Rim Country — loosely defined as "the area some distance back from the rim, both on top and below it" — include the establishment of a dominant culture from approximately A.D. 300 to about 1450 by the Hohokam, and subsequently, the mystifying abandonment of this area by the Hohokam, Mogollon and Anasazi near the end of the 14th century; the appearance of the first Spanish conquistador, Coronado, in 1540; migration of Apaches from the east and Yavapai from the northwest 100 years later; discovery of valuable minerals during the early 1860s, which led to conflicts between prospectors and Indians, and eventually, the construction of Fort Verde; Gen. George Crook's construction of a rough road up and along the rim in 1872; and in response to the rapid depletion of natural resources, the designation of forested "reserves" by the federal government in 1891. This action by the government laid the foundation for the eventual creation of Coconino National Forest, Tonto National Forest and Apache-Sitgreaves National Forest, collectively considered Rim Country's most valuable resource.

Today, Rim Country is much different, of course. Instead of Indian hunters, Spanish explorers and prospectors, the people roving this geological wonder are campers, fishermen, artists, or residents of congested metropolitan areas simply seeking a little peace and quiet, perhaps.

For the people who live in Sedona, or visit here, the Mogollon Rim is a hands-on refuge for enjoying the fresh rains and waterfalls of spring, warm breezes and wildflowers of summer, scurrying wildlife and brightly colored leaves of fall, and beautiful snow-covered rocks, trees and meadows of winter — sometimes, it seems, all in the same day. In fact, the rim offers this community an unusual distinction with regard to the weather; this is a place where people don't just talk about it, they do something about it. They go to the top of the "muggy-own"!

Could this be Sedona?

Throbbing, springtime waterfalls adorn massive walls of rock that mark the Mogollon Rim.

Fall comes a little earlier near the crest of the Mogollon Rim.

Peaceful meadows and thick forests invite a lazy pace on top of the rim.

The snow-capped San Francisco Peaks rise above the rim's colorful, distinctive layers of stone.

A spectacular winter day on the Mogollon Rim.

CHAPTER FOUR

Quite ideally, Sedona is surrounded by the majestic, 2 million-acre Coconino National Forest, which ranges from a 3,000-foot elevation along the Verde River to a height of approximately 13,000 feet on top of the San Francisco Peaks. This unusual contrast of elevation in a span of only 50 miles accounts for the presence of exceptionally varied plant and animal life. Indeed, it causes strange "bedfellows" in the immediate Sedona area, which is midway between Camp Verde and Flagstaff.

For example, snakes, roadrunners and javelina share a "border" with deer, elk and black bear — and agave, cactus and piñon trees almost touch roots and branches with juniper and ponderosa pine. Indeed, this area is a botanical and zoological wonderland.

The magnificent national forest that touches the limits of this city is an invaluable asset; it is an amenity with unmeasurable impact. And it is much more! — because the geologically unique arrangement of valleys, canyons, rims and mountains in this part of Arizona caused the creation of extremely varied and unusually rugged terrain in this beloved forest. As a consequence, some sites have very limited accessibility. Thus, they are marked by virtually being undeveloped — or better, perhaps, they are *unmarked* by the construction of roads, campgrounds and service facilities — and in 1984, the federal government decreed that the largest of these parcels were to be identified as wilderness areas to be left undisturbed, forever escaping the construction of rough, dirt roads so familiar in other national forest areas.

This act effectively created the special, protected parts of Coconino National Forest so enjoyed by outdoor enthusiasts who prefer a very basic recreational experience, and by naturalists who particularly appreciate the "do not disturb" element.

The enjoyment of precious wilderness areas was enhanced further by the fact that the government's 14-year-old decree stipulates that these areas will not have developed amenities other than a few trail signs, and the use of motorized vehicles — even mountain bikes — is not permitted. Hiking, hunting, fishing and horseback riding is allowed; however, it should be known that the people who enjoy these activities in wilderness areas employ considerable precaution, including the use of maps, compasses and other navigational aids.

Fortunately for Sedona — the endowment bestowed on this community almost is unbelievable — the government established 10 wilderness areas that totally or partially are in Coconino National Forest. And of more importance locally, three of these sites — among the most spectacular! — are managed by Sedona Ranger District.

By size, Sycamore Canyon, Red Rock Secret Mountain and Munds Mountain wilderness areas rank 1, 2 and 3 — by spectacular beauty, it's a tie. Residents of Sedona probably would pick Red Rock Secret Mountain Wilderness Area as their favorite, however, because of its close proximity — bordering the city limits in some places — and extensive offering of hiking trails, including West Fork, which might be the most enchanting pathway of all.

Sycamore Canyon Wilderness Area, 55,937 acres of brightly colored cliffs and towering pinnacles, also features a rare, desert-riparian habitat. Essentially, this area includes Sycamore Canyon in its entirety — from forests on the Mogollon Rim to the high desert in Verde Valley.

Red Rock Secret Mountain Wilderness Area encompasses 43,950 acres of buttes, arches and slot canyons beautifully sculpted by wind and water. The trails in this spectacular wilderness climb from deep gorges to high cliffs with magnificent, panoramic views, and in some remote spots, they pass by mysterious, ancient ruins. The spout of landmark Coffeepot Rock hangs over the boundary of this area.

The relatively small — *just* 18,150 acres — Munds Mountain Wilderness Area, which is conveniently located close to Sedona and Village of Oakcreek, extends from the bottoms of Jacks, Woods and Rattlesnake canyons to the tops of Munds and Lee mountains. Also, it features two of Red Rock Country's best-known, picturesque formations, Courthouse and Bell rocks.

For the sheer pleasure of experiencing the fascinating intimacy of an almost-junglelike wilderness, however, it's back to West Fork, spectacularly situated north of Sedona in Oak Creek Canyon. With each rounding of a bend in the trail at West Fork there is an excitement about what is next — especially in the fall, when the brilliant reds and oranges, soft pinks and yellows, and warm browns and bronzes that mean winter is coming decorate this magnificent, massive vent.

Here, the beauty of this pristine canyon, formed by a now-serene stream that is the only significant tributary of Oak Creek, beckons hikers with a compelling allure not unlike the seductive singing of ancient, mythological sea nymphs. These hikers are entranced by steep, red-rock walls curiously created from sandstone deposited in the dunes of a prehistoric desert; vast, thick patches of ferns; and giant grapevines that wrap scraggly stems around the trunks and branches of enormous pines, adding an almost-frightening mystique to this somewhat-eerie wilderness. In other areas of this storybook land, a lush undercover is composed of beautiful wildflowers like buttercup, columbine, larkspur and Indian paintbrush complemented by blackberries and grapes, horsetail reeds and even miniature roses.

As visitors are pulled farther into this wonderful canyon, crossing the perennial creek that gives this trail so much character at least a dozen times, they are delighted by a continually more-abundant display of rich, riparian vegetation. And they are stunned by this surprising land where a marvelous mix of natural forces dating back to the days when this continent collided with Europe, Africa and South America to form the giant super-continent of Pangaea, has produced mesmerizing combinations of wildlife. This is scenic wilderness in its ultimate glory!

Slot canyons are a trademark of wilderness areas.

Wild, as in wilderness — and a wonder, as in wonderful!

Green, brown, red —

and gold abound!

Wilderness areas feature art by nature.

The lure of West Fork is obvious.

Natural lace —

and reflected glimmer.

Thick patches of fern add mystique to a somewhat-eerie wilderness.

In West Fork, too —

seasons change almost overnight.

Icicles and "plantcicles"!

Pretty cold. Also, cold and pretty.

CHAPTER FIVE

Just as the creek-rich, red-rock canyons of Sedona and the surrounding wilderness areas attract people today, numerous Indian cultures were drawn to this beautiful land centuries ago. The history of these early Native Americans extends over a period of approximately 1,400 years, starting in A.D. 1 and ending, mysteriously, about A.D. 1425.

Though the interpretation and chronological classification of what occurred during this historic period often is altered, or even discarded because of new evidence, it generally is conceded that the ancient cliff dwellings found in the Sedona area were constructed during The Honanki Phase, A.D. 1130-1300, when an influx of Sinagua increased the population of this red-rock region. Indeed, many archaeologists attribute the introduction of an architectural style that employed masonry construction to these people.

As with so many of Sedona's attractive features, the two largest cliff dwellings in this intriguing area have been labeled "world class" by learned authorities. These ancient ruins, named Palatki and Honanki, probably were occupied by Sinagua people between A.D. 1130 and A.D. 1280. Justification for assessing this time frame is based on a date determined by examining potsherds and the tree rings of wooden lintels, which were used for support over a door or window.

The theory crediting the construction of these handsome dwellings to Sinagua who emigrated from the Flagstaff area is endorsed by the majority of archaeologists; others, however, relate the occupation of Sedona's canyons to a climate that was exceptionally warm and moist, thus attracting members of the Southern Sinagua culture who already were inhabitants of the Verde Valley.

Palatki and Honanki first were reported by Dr. Jesse Walter Fewkes of the Smithsonian Institute in 1895. Later, in 1911, Fewkes conducted test excavations at these sites while investigating Hopi migration. It was this early archaeologist who named these ruins Palatki and Honanki, Hopi words that mean "Red House" and "Bear House," respectively.

Palatki is composed of two separated pueblos, which suggests that two families lived here. Supporting this theory are circular, shieldlike pictographs that some experts contend are clan symbols. The eastern pueblo, which is the largest, shows evidence of population growth by the addition of two rooms. The western pueblo features a kiva, or meeting room, indicated by the presence of a raised bench.

Originally, Honanki had as many as 60 rooms and a very large collection of pictographs. Unfortunately, many of these rooms and pictographs have been destroyed by pothunters, vandals and the aging process imposed by time. Nonetheless, the mysterious aura pervading Honanki is thick with excitement, causing challenging speculation.

Officials at the Sedona Ranger District are charged with stewardship of the Palatki and Honanki ruins, which are extremely popular curiosities for area visitors. This assignment requires the careful blending of contrasting interests; that is, these officials are faced with preserving the scientific value of these important sites, and at the same time, making them available for public enjoyment — not an easy task. Conscientious visitors can support the ranger district's attempt to satisfy both responsibilities by subscribing to a simple creed: Don't change anything, don't take anything and don't leave anything!

Though Palatki and Honanki are the best-known cliff dwellings in this area, there are numerous other spectacular ruins tucked into beautiful sites in caves and on ledges throughout the wilderness areas of this region. Informed residents and visitors know of obvious sites in Boynton Canyon, for example, and other ruins are situated in passes and adjacent to washes where popular hiking trails are located. Fact is, however, it is best not to search for secluded, unidentified ruins, which have great scientific value; ideally, visitors will satisfy their curiosity by visiting Palatki and Honanki, where the expectation and accommodation of visitors is evident.

With regard to the aforementioned pictographs, these drawings and paintings *on* rock surfaces constitute one-half of a categorical term used to describe ancient forms of communication popularly referred to as "rock art." The other half is composed of carvings and peckings *in* rock surfaces, called petroglyphs.

The difference between pictographs and petroglyphs essentially is the same as what separates drawing from carving. In fact, picto, from the Latin prefix "pictus," when added to graph, refers to a pictured object used to convey an idea or information. Similarly, petro and glyph, from the Greek prefixes "petra" and "glyphe," mean rock and carving, respectively. Thus, drawings on in-place rock surfaces are called pictographs, and carvings on these same surfaces are called petroglyphs.

It is reported that rock art is common in eastern Utah, the Grand Canyon, Canyon de Chelly and the Sedona area — but it is uncommon, even rare, elsewhere. Once again, Sedona is fortunately endowed!

Most ancient dwellings in this area are circa A.D. 1130 - 1300.

In Hopi language, Palatki, a two-pueblo complex, means "Red House."

Situated at the base of a massive red-rock wall, Honanki had as many as 60 rooms.

Honanki is a Hopi word that means "Bear House."

Pictographs are drawings and paintings *on* rock.

Petroglyphs are carvings and peckings *in* rock.

Numerous spectacular ruins are tucked into caves —

and perched on ledges throughout the wilderness areas of this region.

In part, the age of ancient ruins is determined by examining wooden supports —

and by studying potsherds discovered at various sites.

CHAPTER SIX

Much is written and said about how uniquely Sedona is situated in northern Arizona; in reality, how uniquely Sedona is situated *in the Southwest* would be a more-appropriate assessment. It is not an exaggeration to count this community's "neighborhood" among the most beautiful and interesting in the world. Especially, for the adventurous people who are unabashedly romanced by the geology and history of the 150,000-square-mile Colorado Plateau.

According to geologists, the Sedona and Oak Creek Canyon landscape has been more than 350 million years in the making. As a result of this unfathomable process, Oak Creek and its canyon are carved into the southern margin of the Colorado Plateau, and Sedona is positioned immediately at the base of this vast plateau — here, called the Mogollon Rim.

To the north and northeast, spread across the Colorado Plateau, are Sedona's attractive neighbors — phenomena like the San Francisco Peaks and the Grand Canyon; Vermilion Cliffs and Buckskin Gulch in the Paria Canyon-Vermilion Cliffs Wilderness Area; White Mesa Natural Bridge, Grand Falls, Keet Seel and Betatkin ruins, Canyon de Chelly, Monument Valley and the Painted Desert, all on the Navajo Indian Reservation; plus numerous other monuments, various national forests and a rich assortment of additional wilderness areas.

No wonder people think Sedona is "uniquely situated" — and isn't the credibility of this appraisal obvious as you ponder the following geologic resumés, just a sampling of the plateau's exceptional environmental amenities?

• The 13,000-foot San Francisco Peaks possess an unusual, but beloved, character. Because "The Peaks" constitute a solo act, so to speak, with balanced simplicity accompanied by artful design, they were described by early explorers as "the most beautiful mountain — not *mountains* — ever seen." Still, this lonely mountain is capable of dramatic statements and fierce moods.

• The Grand Canyon, born of powerful erosion and faulting, is situated in the southwestern quadrant of the Colorado Plateau. More specifically, the canyon is carved through an area called the Kaibab Plateau, which was formed when this portion of the Colorado Plateau was uplifted — not evenly, because the canyon's north rim is 1,000 feet higher than its south rim. This uplifting created a 1,500-square-mile area on the north rim that is a mile above the surrounding high-desert and is blanketed by the Kaibab National Forest.

• The Navajo Indian Reservation, where the Little Colorado River tumbles over stark-but-beautiful Grand Falls, is the largest remnant of Native American land in this country. In fact, its 25,000-square-mile area is larger than several states, and its range of elevations features sudden changes, including Black Mesa's sharp rise to 1,500 feet above Chinle Valley. Also, its spectacular, Southwestern-style landforms, such as White Mesa Natural Bridge and those that punctuate Monument Valley and Canyon de Chelly, are well-known.

THE PLATEAU

• Amazingly, it is said that a hike through the 40-mile-long canyon in the Paria Canyon-Vermilion Cliffs Wilderness Area constitutes a tour through 200 million years of geologic time. Geologists also say that dinosaurs roamed the earth when the rocks that now form the walls of Paria Canyon were deep layers of silt and ooze beneath an inland sea. The respected — it can be a dangerous place — hallmark of Paria Canyon is Buckskin Gulch, a deep and narrow gorge described as "a twisting, rock-walled labyrinth characterized by natural stairwells, caves and arches." In places, this gorge is less than two feet wide and undulating walls block views of the sky.

Some neighborhood!

In general terms, the Colorado Plateau — part of Arizona, Utah, Colorado and New Mexico — is bounded by the Wasatch and Uinta mountains on the north, the Mogollon Rim and Sedona on the south, the western slope of the Rocky Mountains on the east, and an expansive region of basins and ranges on the west. The landscape of this massive area is stunning, exhibiting the geologic and biologic diversity ordinarily associated with continents. A familiar exclamation — "You have to see it to believe it!" — is applicable. The invitation extended by this land, however, is related to more than natural beauty; numerous historians have cited intangible, almost-spiritual qualities. These scholars and noted writers refer to the Colorado Plateau as though it was alive, even mentioning the soul of this mysterious place, which they accept as an archaeological treasure — and they describe the plateau as "America's last great wilderness" for reasons ascribed to human traits, not just physical elements. Here, people feel a sense of freedom and adventure that is not unlike what apparently is enjoyed by the soaring eagles, swooping ravens and darting wrens that inhabit this wild plateau.

Because of *the plateau* — a land where the grandest canyon in the world is mentioned among other amenities; where attractions are so plentiful, the favorite of visitors is as varied as the people who visit; where often, even seeing is not believing — and *the red rocks, the canyon, the rim, the ruins* and *the wilderness,* Sedona is, indeed, the most uniquely beautiful site on Earth!

Rogers Lake, southwest of Flagstaff, reflects the majestic San Francisco Peaks.

In the fall, "The Peaks" are brightly colored with millions of quaking aspens.

Golden "pompons" salute Vermilion Cliffs on the boundary of Paria Plateau —

which features haunting slot canyons like Buckskin Gulch.

Sunrise and sunset illuminate White Mesa Natural Bridge —

and Grand Falls, respectively, on the vast Navajo Indian Reservation.

From the South Rim, the Grand Canyon exhibits mesmerizing moods —

and captivating colors.

Thunder Falls, inside the Grand Canyon, is a surprise.

Wotan's Throne, from the North Rim, is an awesome sight!

Sedon*ah!*

Special thanks!

Noreen, Marcia and Michelle Johnson
John Johnson and George Getz
Dave Tate and Donn Frye
Dennis Webster, *Land O' Sun Printers*
Bill Martin and Suzanne Walters, *American Color*
Mary Ann Small, *Image Craft*
Judy Harper, *Proofreader*